UTAMARO

by Sadao Kikuchi

translated by
Myra Fraser
&
Masaaki Tanaka

edited by
Don Kenny

CONTENTS

(Cover Photo) Detail of Woman with a Glass Toy, one of 'Ten Features of Women'

UTAMARO

by Sadao Kikuchi

translated by Myra Fraser & Masaaki Tanaka

edited by Don Kenny

© All rights reserved. No. 30 of Hoikusha's Color Books Series. Published by Hoikusha Publishing Co., Ltd. 17-13, 1-chome, Uemachi, Higashi-ku, Osaka, 540 Japan. Book Code Number 0171-540030-7700. First Edition in 1974. Fourth Edition in 1979. Printed in JAPAN

2 — Summer in Takanawa Diptych

'Enjoying the Elegant Fragrance of Flowers'

3

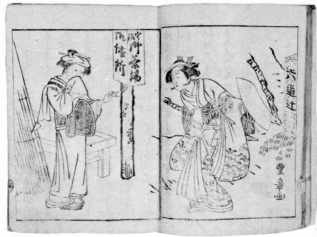

3 — Illustration for the Humorous Novel titled 'Keepsake'

Utamaro's Début

Although the date is not exactly clear, in his youth Utamaro became a disciple of the famous artist Toriyama Sekien. His first pen name was Kitagawa Toyoaki and this signature is found on the cover illustration of a Bunraku Puppet *Jôruri* Script titled *Forty-Eight Ways to Succeed in Love*, published in November 1775. He was then twenty-three, and this is considered one of his earliest works. In 1776 he made a larger print using only black ink, which was published in *Actor's Memorial Haiku for Ichikawa Goryû*. The signature Toyoaki printed on the actor's portrait done on a narrow woodblock indicates that Utamaro had begun gaining ground as an Ukiyoe artist by this time. The picture shown above was an illustration he did for a comic novelette titled *Keepsake* published in 1779.

Doing book illustrations and portraits of Kabuki actors was the usual thing young artists of that time did before becoming known in the world of Ukiyoe art. Utamaro was no exception.

4 — Kabuki Actor Yoshizawa Iroha
as Osato of the Sushi Shop

5 — Diptych titled 'The Foot of Ryôgoku Bridge'

6 —
Brocade of Daily Life
in Yamashita

7 —
Diptych titled 'Court S[e]
and Dance Gathering'

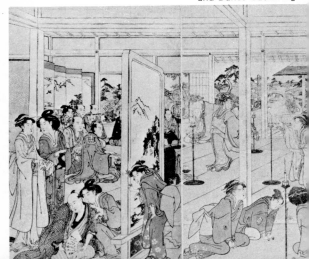

Production of Beautiful Woman Prints Begun

He took the pen name Utamaro in 1781 and began to draw increasingly more portraits of Beautiful Women in single figure pictures while continuing production of book illustrations and actors portraits as before. The print seen to the left is one of his earliest Beautiful Woman prints.

Utamaro's Beautiful Woman prints were first produced in sets of two or three in large sized color prints as seen in Plates 2, 5 and 7. This style of print set was originated by Torii Kiyonaga who was the most popular Ukiyoe artist of the Tenmei Era (1781-1788).

Kiyonaga drew realistic, healthy and stately figures of beautiful women with an elegant touch in bright colors. His beauties are in most cases drawn in groups so as to be all the more impressive. Dress designs are so minutely detailed that they evoke a realistic feeling and there is good harmony between the figures and backgrounds. Utamaro learned from Kiyonaga's Beautiful Woman prints.

青樓仁和嘉女藝者部

大万度

萩江
おいよ
竹次

哥麿画

8 — Entertainers Dressing near a Large Lantern to perform
at the Niwaka Festival in the Gay Quarters

10

9 — One of 'Entertainers at the Niwaka Festival in the Gay Quarters'

Pleasure Quarter Series

Utamaro gained wide experience in a variety of types of prints including actor portraits, Beautiful Women, landscapes, and illustrations of popular books. He then began to draw pictures of life in the licensed pleasure quarters, for which French novelist Edmond de Goncourt (1822-1896) later called him a "brothel artist." Plates 8, 10 and 11 are works of his brothel series. It is interesting that these entertainers are dressed up to join the annual event of Mazaki Tenman Shrine in the Shin-Yoshiwara district. This event was called *Niwaka*, which means impromptu, improvisational, or spontaneous.

10 (below left) — Three Beauties of the Pleasure Quarters
11 (below right) — Women Dressed for the Kashima Dance at the Niwaka Festival

12 — The Niwaka Festival, an Illustration from
'A Picture Book of Annual Events in the
Yoshiwara Pleasure Quarters'

The entertainers in these prints are listed in the book titled
A Close Look at Yoshiwara, which described the Yoshiwara
district and included a map, names of courtesans and prostitutes, holidays, etc. According to this book the *Niwaka Brothel
Entertainer* series is said to have been done in the early Tenmei
Era. The last character of Utamaro's signature in this series is in
vermilion and it is thought that this indicates that he gained
confidence as a Beautiful Woman artist at this time.

13 (left) — The Courtesan Ochie of Koise-ya Teahouse
14 (above) — Toyohina of the Tomimoto Teahouse

15

Late Tenmei through Early Kansei Style

From the late Tenmei Era through the early Kansei Era (1789-1800), Utamaro produced prints under the patronage of the publisher Tsutaya Jûzaburô, in association with Enjû, a famous comic story writer. Most of his best illustration work was produced during this period. Good examples appear in a picture book of comic *tanka* poems, titled *Waka Ebisu* published in 1786 by Tsutaya, *Picture Book of Edo Sparrows*, and *Picture Book of Selected Insects* (1788), an illustration from which is seen in Plate 15. *Waka Ebisu* is said to be his first illustration work for a comic picture book.

15 — Illustration from the 'Picture Book of Selected Insects'

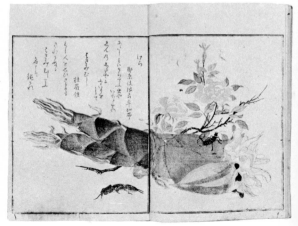

16 — Illustration from 'Thousands
of Birds'

During the same time Utamaro also drew illustrations for a large color print book titled *Thousands of Birds* (published in 1789 by Tsutaya) which makes a good pair with the *Picture Book of Selected Insects*. These contain masterpiece sketches of flowers, birds and insects. All of these picture books demonstrate Utamaro's keen powers of observation and excellent sketching technique. It can be said that it was his long-trained observing eye that enabled him to create such unique genre pictures later.

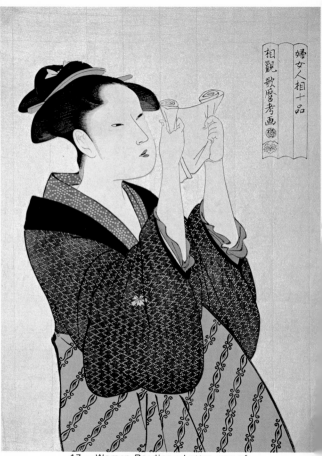

婦女人相十品

相觀　歌麿考畫

17 — Woman Reading a Letter, one of
'Ten Features of Women'

18 — Woman with a Glass Toy, one of 'Ten Features of Women'

婦女人相十品

相観 歌麿考画

19 (above left) — Woman with a Parasol, one of
'Ten Features of Women'
20 (above right) — Beauty with a Pipe, one of
'Ten Features of Women'

Close-up Portraits of Beautiful Women

During the Tenmei Era Utamaro was greatly influenced by the styles of Kitao Shigemasa (1740-1820) and Torii Kiyonaga (1752-1815). But he introduced his own new style of close-up portraits of Beautiful Women at the beginning of the Kansei Era. He used the idea of the close-up portraits of Kabuki actors which had first been done by Katsukawa Shunshô (1726-1792) who not only depicted the features of the actors in close-up but also their expressions during performance.

Utamaro made use of the merits of this close-up portrait style to draw his ideal beauty. Utamaro also applied the technique of a mica background to his Beautiful Woman prints. This technique had been used for the background coloring of actor close-ups. Plates 13 and 14 both depict renowned women in Edo in the early Kansei Era. Utamaro thus made portraits of real women of his time as well as drawing his ideal beauties of various kinds as seen in Plates 17-20 and 23-25.

21 —
KATSUKAWA
SHUNSHÔ
Actor
Ichikawa Danjûrô V
as Kudô,
one of
'Fan Pictures
of Edo'

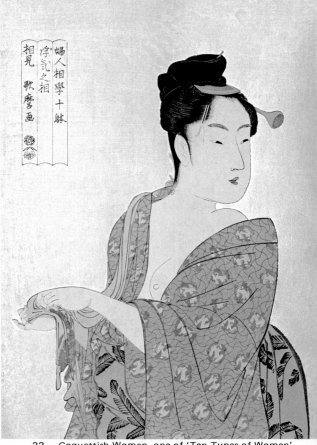

婦人相學十躰
浮気之相
相見　歌麿画

22 — Coquettish Woman, one of 'Ten Types of Women'

婦人相學十躰

相見

歌麿画

23 — Woman with a Fan, one of 'Ten Types of Women'

24 —
Amusing Woman,
one of
'Ten Types of Women'

Characteristics of Utamaro's Beautiful Woman Prints

The two series seen in Plates 17-20 and 23-25 were produced during 1790 and 1791. All his women are slightly round-faced with a full jawline — his concept of ideal beauty. Unlike his preceding works that have many lines, the number of lines in these series was reduced to the least possible. Utamaro even simplified the facial outlines and designs of dresses which were previously depicted more elaborately. A certain stylization appears in these works completing his concept of ideal beauty.

Restricting the use of colors, he not only displayed the beauty of his models but also tried to depict their sensuousness by the use of the juxtaposition of color planes without outlines. Here Utamaro achieved a new type of Beautiful Woman print which had not existed previously.

25 —
Woman Counting
on her Fingers,
one of
'Ten Types
of Women'

当世踊子揃　通成之

哥麿筆

26 — Dance Called Dôjô-ji, one of 'Collection of Dancers'

27 — Three Celebrated Beauties

28 (left) — Dance Called Sparrows at Yoshiwara,
one of 'Collection of Dancers'
29 (right) — Dance of the Heron Maiden, one of
'Collection of Dancers'

Expression of Emotion in the Utamaro Style

It is often said that Utamaro's women all look alike. At first
sight this seems true because he drew his concept of ideal
beauty. However, if we look closely at Plate 27 we can see
subtle distinctions in their features. We can tell by the family
crests on their kimonos and fans that they are Naniwa-ya
Okita, Tomimoto Toyohina and Takashima Ohisa (from right
to left), who were all famous beauties of Edo in the Kansei
Era. Utamaro gave them distinctive faces by slightly changing

the line of their eyebrows, eyes, noses, etc. These subtle distinctions become more noticeable when seen in the same print.

Plate 30 is a novel example showing differences in women's hair styles in Edo (present Tokyo), Kyoto, and Osaka at that time.

30 —
Customs of
Beauties from
Mikanotsu

31 — Triptych Called 'Needlework'

32 — Diptych Called 'Women in the Kitchen'

Full Length Figure Prints

Utamaro resumed production of full length figure prints af
his success with the close-up portraits which had made him
number one Ukiyoe artist of the Kansei Era. The daily activit
of housewives were taken as subject matter for Plates 31 and
These examples are from sets of two or three with two figure
each piece. The beauty of the group rather than individ
beauty is stressed in these works. Of the three pieces in Plate
the left-hand picture is the best in composition. It display
mother looking through a piece of cloth with her child play
around her knees.

This would also be an excellent work as an independent print. In the other two pieces, related to each other by the line of the cloth, there is some degree of stylization in the postures and especially the positions of the legs of the women. The amount of bare skin shown adds a quality of decadence to the total impression. This triptych was originally designed so that any one of the pieces could be enjoyed by itself or the whole scene could be enjoyed somewhat like a puzzle when they were linked together in a set. It somehow lacks interest as a total picture, but it reflects Utamaro's skillful technique in handling a large sized print. By setting a girl with an insect cage behind her mother in black in the middle picture and placing a boy teasing a cat with a mirror in front of his sister in the right picture, Utamaro not only gave variety to the composition but also a sense of perspective. All these aspects show Utamaro's excellent artistic ability.

33 —
Under a Willow Tree

娘日時計 巳刻

哥麿筆

34 — Hour of the Serpent (10 a.m.), one of
'Maidens of the Hours'

Plate 36   Plate 37

Innovations in 'Maidens of the Hours'

Utamaro was not content with drawing only external beauty like the beauty of facial features, sensuous figures and costumes. He also tried to imply inner emotions through facial expressions. He even contrived to express the softness and luster of women's skin in the series seen in Plates 34-38.

In the production of woodblock prints, usually the primary work is making black ink outlines. Woodblocks for the colors are then prepared according to the number of necessary colors. Drawing of black outlines is thus the elementary business of the artist in making an Ukiyoe print. This technique is adequate for expressing a rough sketch of a face, but black outlines were

時計申ノ刻

36 — Hour of the Ram
 (2 p.m.), one of
 'Maidens of the Hours'
37 — Hour of the Dragon
 (8 a.m.), one of
 'Maidens of the Hours'
38 — Hour of the Monkey
 (4 p.m.), one of
 'Maidens of the Hours'

Plate 38

not suitable for the subtle qualitative details of skin that Utamaro wished to convey. Thus he gave up the use of outlines and instead used the juxtaposition of different colors to delineate features. He depicted the fair, tender skin of his women by using a special white print paper from Fukui Prefecture contrasted with a background of crushed yellow pigment. In Plate 34 he used an actual outline for the neckline but drew the nose with a special ridge line technique called *kiwamedashi*, in which a non-colored line mounting is pushed up from the back side of the paper. Thus Utamaro employed an advanced technique to draw out the beauty of his models.

39 — The Mirror, one of 'Seven Women
Making Up at Mirrors'

高嶌おひさ　高嶌おひさ

40 — Ohisa of the Takashima-ya Teahouse

Drawing Popular Women

Plates 39 and 42 were done in the both-side print technique where the front view of a model is printed on one side of the paper and the back view on the other. This technique was used by Utamaro to portray the qualities of these women as seen from both back and front, right and left.

Utamaro utilized the idea of the both-side print for Plate 41. Ohisa's lovely face appears in the mirror while her slightly dishevelled, sensual back view completes the expression of her charms. Utamaro devoted himself to the study of these beauties and won his fame through them.

42 — Okita, Daughter of the Teashop Naniwa-ya

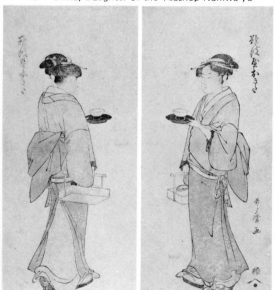

43 — Couple by a Standing Screen

44 — Inside and Outside a Mosquito Net

45 — Diptych titled 'Two Pillows'

Woodblock Engraving and Printing Craftsmanship

Plates 43-45 represent Utamaro's works with scenes of love. In these pictures a unique technique of printing which plays an important part in giving a special atmosphere to the finished pictures is fully demonstrated. Plate 43 shows a woman peering through a young man's *haori* coat of silk gauze, adding an interesting coyness to the picture as a whole. In Plate 44 the man is inside the net — set up around the bedding — looking out. Such works were only possible through the use of a color overlapping technique which is peculiar to Ukiyoe woodblock prints. By using the mosquito net and silk gauze, Utamaro expressed these love scenes in a subtle, indirect, muted way, which tends to create a more erotic atmosphere than a blatant, obvious picture of lovemaking would. It is erotic while still in good taste.

The mosquito net is printed with two blocks with lines at different angles so as to present the intercrossing net lines in the final printing and allow the man inside to show through. The elaborate craftsmanship of the block engraver is definitely important here just as it is in the hair lines in the close-up portraits. The openwork of the *haori* coat shows the excellent technique of the printer.

歌撰戀之部

お思恋

46 (above) — Reverie of Love, one of 'Poems of Love'
47 (right) — Beauty with a Comb

Comparison between Van Gogh and Utamaro

Utamaro's Beautiful Woman prints gradually became stylized as a result of the development of his ideal type and with his increased skill. Probably Utamaro noticed this himself. The use of cloth designs for the background in Plates 47 and 49 presents a different atmosphere from his earlier close-up works most of which have white mica or crushed yellow backgrounds.

Plate 48 is a painting by Vincent Van Gogh titled "The Nanny." In it Van Gogh used a floral print background, showing a parallel with Utamaro's cloth design background. It is a commonly held opinion among world art experts that Japan's

Ukiyoe art greatly influenced the French post-impressionists. Some even say Van Gogh based his work on Utamaro's. However, a hasty conclusion regarding Utamaro's background treatment being directly imported into Van Gogh's works would be wrong. There are many examples of European portraits that display a model with a curtain backdrop. Another common feature of these works is the half-length treatment of the model, which is common in Oriental portraits particularly those of Buddhist priests. But this feature too is common in European portraits.

49 —
Beauty
with an
Insect Cage

50 — Tatsumi Roko, one of 'Six Celebrated Beauties'

51 — Widow of the House of Asahi, one of
'Six Celebrated Beauties'

51

Plate 52

Plate 54

Plate 53

Plate 55

52 — Ohisa of the Takashima-ya
       Teahouse, one of
       'Six Celebrated Beauties'
53 — Okita of the Naniwa-ya
       Teahouse, one of
       'Six Celebrated Beauties'
54 — Toyohina of the Tomimoto
       Teahouse, one of
       'Six Celebrated Beauties'
55 — Osen of the Ôgi-ya
       Teahouse, one of
       'Six Celebrated Beauties'
56 — Kuronushi, one of
       'Six Elegant Poets'

Plate 56

'Six Celebrated Beauties'

Utamaro did many of his best Beautiful Woman close-ups in the middle of the Kansei Era. This series is different from previous works in its delicate delineation of hair lines. This detailed treatment of hair was of course Utamaro's intention but its actual printing would never have been possible but for the superior skill of the engravers whose names can no longer be identified.

Plates 52-55, 57 and 58 comprise the entire series.

57 — The Courtesan Somenosuke of the Matsuba-ya
Teahouse, one of 'Popular Beauties'

54

当時全盛美人揃

兵庫座内
花妻
はなつま

哥麿筆

59 —
The Courtesan Komurasaki
of the Tama-ya Teahouse,
one of 'Popular Beauties'

'Popular Beauties'

Utamaro made a series of the most prosperous courtesans belonging to the highest class houses in the Shin-Yoshiwara pleasure quarters. He drew these women in three-quarter length. In such a composition the figure appears to extend outside of the panel thus giving much more vigor to the figure as well as a feeling of fullness to the entire print.

Such looking-back poses as those in Plates 57 and 58 lead our eyes to the space outside the picture. The position and shape of the knee in Plate 58 seems to be typical of Utamaro.

Her straight back and well-proportioned, balanced arms twisting a letter before her make this an impressive posture study. Utamaro tried to draw out the inner emotions of these women. He has depicted Komurasaki's embarrassed, coquettish look in Plate 59 by placing an intentionally small pipe in a hand almost concealed by the sleeve in an otherwise well-balanced composition and by the large sash tied in front.

60 (below left) — The Courtesan Shizuka of the Tama-ya
Teahouse, one of 'Popular Beauties'
61 (below right) — The Courtesan Jakusui of the Wakamatsu-ya
Teahouse, one of 'Popular Beauties'

62 — The Entertainer Kamekichi, one of
'Five Poems about Women'

59

64 —
The Tama River
at Koya, one of
'Scenes on
Six Tama Rivers'

Change of Style

Of the *Six Tama Rivers* series, three are extant. They are seen in Plates 63-65. Note the face line of the close-up in color. Vermilion lines were used for the face contours in this series to give a sense of soft skin just as the juxtaposition of color without outlines was applied for the same purpose in the *Maidens of the Hours* series. A vermilion line gives a milder feeling than a black line and so has succeeded in making the women depicted in this period more impressive. The movement seen in the eyes and hands of these women also helps make the facial lines more effective.

In contrast to the fine structural composition of Plate 63, an extreme stylization is noted in Plate 64 in the expression of the neck line as well as the excessively sloping shoulders. This is an example of the somewhat lower quality work Utamaro did for a short while during this period.

65 —
The Courtesan
Hinazuru of
the Chôji-ya
Teahouse,
one of
'Scenes on
Six Tama
Rivers'

青樓十二時　續

歌麿筆

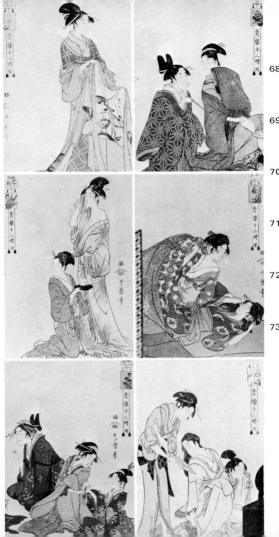

68 (above left) — Hour of the Hare (6 a.m.)
69 (middle left) — Hour of the Snake (10 a.m.)
70 (bottom left) — Hour of the Ram (2 p.m.)
71 (above right) — Hour of the Tiger (4 a.m.)
72 (middle right) — Hour of the Dragon (8 a.m.)
73 (bottom right) — Hour of the Horse (Noon)

74 —
(above left)
Hour of
the Cock
(6 p.m.)
75 —
(below left)
Hour of
the Boar
(10 p.m.)
76 —
(above right)
Hour of
the Monkey
(4 p.m.)
77 —
(below right)
Hour of
the Dog
(8 p.m.)

'Twelve Hours in the Gay Quarters'

In Plate 67 the upside-down sandal is an especially interesting touch. Utamaro's keen sense of observation and his boldness in depicting a prostitute leaving her bed blear-eyed to go to the toilet at 2 a.m. are strongly evident here. Note that she is carrying paper and an incense stick, either to ward off mosquitoes or to disguise unpleasant odors.

78 — Girl with a Letter from Kiri, one of
'Five North Country Hues'

79 — Teahouse Woman in Shinagawa

80 (above left) —
Riverbank (Kawagishi) Prostitute, one of
'Five North Country Hues'

81 (above right) —
One Shot (Teppô) Prostitute, one of
'Five North Country Hues'

'Five North Country Hues'

Shin-Yoshiwara had not only high class courtesans belongin
to larger brothels like Ôgi-ya and Matsuba-ya but also variou
classes of lower prositutes who belonged to smaller pleasur
houses visited by people of corresponding economic mean
These various lower class prostitutes were used as models in th
Five North Country Hues series. The woman in Plate 78, from
middle-class brothel, is enjoying a pleasant letter from a man. I
her gestures of delight she appears to be a naive young girl fa
removed from the world of prostitutes. Utamaro's style ofte
allows us to see prostitutes as individual human beings rath

than stereotyped images.

In contrast to this woman, those in Plates 80 and 81 convey a decadent atmosphere. They were very low class prostitutes living on the banks of the canal which surrounded the district like a moat. It can be said that Utamaro found beauty in decadence itself in his depiction of the shameless expression of the barebreasted woman in Plate 80 using a toothpick and the lascivious figure of the cheap prostitute in Plate 81 who keeps paper ready between her teeth while she neglectfully displays her full breasts.

82 —
Woman of the
West Station

83 —
Woman Divers
for Abalone

Detail of
Woman Divers
for Abalone

Detail of Woman Divers for Abalone

84 — Woman Divers
for Abalone
at Enoshima

Influence of Feudal Government Policy

The administrative reform in the Kansei Era by the head minister in the Shogun's cabinet, Matsudaira Sadanobu, placed various restrictions on everyday life, and art became subject to censorship. As a result, the range of subjects allowed for Ukiyoe prints became narrower. The seals of government approval seen on Utamaro's prints are examples of the changed circumstances.

Plates 83-85 must have been approved under the condition that they depict the beauty of working women. Using such permissable subjects, Utamaro was able to continue to sketch

85 — Diptych of Woman Divers for Abalone

the physical beauty of women. He used vermilion lines for their healthy bodies to make their figures more impressive. In the center print a woman and child are sketched, ostensibly emphasizing maternal affection in the design. This most probably was only for the sake of passing government censorship.

As seen in the detail on page 70, the engraving of the black hair of the diver with a chisel in her mouth is an elaborate work for a full length figure and shows Utamaro at his artistic zenith.

婦人手業操鏡

喜多川歌麿筆

86 — Reeling Linen Thread, one of 'Women's Skills'
87 (right) — Making Balls, one of 'Twelve Skills of Women'

88 —
Hairdressing,
one of
'Twelve Skills
of Women'

婦人自業拾二工

'Twelve Skills of Women' and 'Women's Skills'

Utamaro took to drawing working women and published two series on this subject. In the series seen in Plates 87 and 88 two women in close-up are arranged in each piece depicting mostly light labor including professionals and housewives. These pictures serve as a good historical reference for studying the everyday labors of those days. Utamaro's ideal image became more oval-faced during this period and has a blank expression compared with the voluptuous atmosphere of the beauties drawn at his peak.

Different from the *Twelve Skills of Women* series the pictures in the *Women's Skills* series are full length figures which evoke a more active atmosphere. The composition of Plate 86 is brief and to the point. The lovely figure of the woman working concentratedly is in impressive bright colors. It is interesting that the flax yarn is shown by a blank space between color planes.

婦人手業操鏡

89 —
Washing,
one of
'Women's Skills'

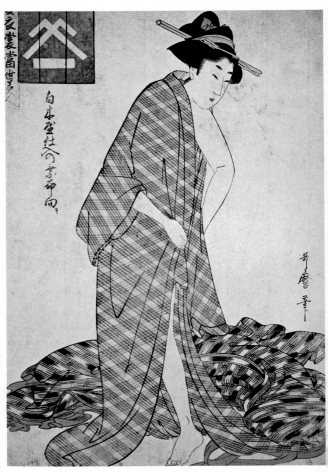

91 (right) — Woman in Summer Costume, one of
'Women in New Utamaro-Style Costumes'

92 (above left) —
Courtesan in Overrobe, one of 'Women in
New Utamaro-Style Costumes'
93 (above right) —
Woman Reading a Letter, one of 'Women in
New Utamaro-Style Costumes'

In Praise of His Own Art

The world of Ukiyoe Beautiful Woman prints of the Kansei
Era was led by Utamaro. It has been discovered that about
forty publishers regularly solicited Utamaro for his drawings at
his peak. Most of Utamaro's contemporaries were more or less
influenced by him or produced prints drawn consciously in his
style. Utamaro then began to write explanations and praise of
his work on his prints as seen in the *Women in New Utamaro-
Style Costumes* series (Plates 91-93).

In this series he contrived to express soft textures by using blank space instead of lines for cloth. In the *Modern Beauties in Summer Dress* series such shop names as Shiroki-ya, Kameya and Daimaru appear from which the material used for the kimono in the picture was bought. The cloth patterns used in this series were popular designs of the day and Utamaro even adds information on the optimum use of the material, such as larger designs, dyeing with white spots, etc. However, the artistry of this series is not as inspired as the idea itself.

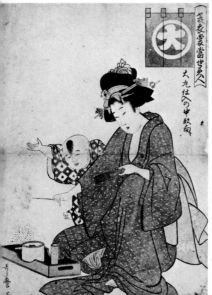

94 —
Material from
the Daimaru,
one of
'Women in New
Utamaro-Style
Costumes'

95 — Delivering a Letter, one of
'Five Elegant Pine Needles'

96 — Oume and Kumenosuke, one of
'Types of Love and Devotion'

Quantity without Quality

Utamaro took themes from stories of double suicides then popular in the Bunraku Puppet *Jôruri* drama for his love story series which he started producing around the middle of the Kansei Era. This may have been influenced by the Tokugawa Government's policy to stress moral teachings to the general public. Perhaps they felt if people could see the miserable plight such excesses could lead to, they would be more restrained in their private lives.

97 (below left) —
Murakumo of the 'Thousand Tales Reflected in the Moon'
98 (below right) — Koharu and Jihei, one of 'Types of
Love and Devotion'

99 —
Parting at
Sunrise,
one of
'Five Elegant
Pine Needles'

Plate 99 is said to have been done during the Kyôwa Era (1801-1804). This close-up print of a couple is very stylized. This is one of the works Utamaro did in a rush during the period of his greatest popularity. With all his creative and expressive talent he could not avoid hasty production of quantities of somewhat inferior works which finally resulting in a general loss of vitality.

おもやつをい

おまへはなもうおれがきいつもこのごろはどういつと
はらたいなんとえまさいうとあのね
子ういふじらふもとつと手たりまんれ
ようよきましうとみつらきてゝれ
いつとらう きみたらさちゃのは
「さヤゝ おまへの
やうなはつ しうこう
つれてあるこでやな
ゆめらしきらんぬきものら
「そらそこへ
こりくおきまんととの
おまへよさへてへの
ういらのとのさちゃよさ
おれて つうとつよく
おかでゝ さののうろく
よれしさう りしつくゝつく
そこへあらゝつて
ようらそのつるけの

100 — A Chatterbox, one of 'Variegated Word Blossoms'

86

俗に云 ぐうたら兵衛

教訓
親の目鑑

101 — A Loafer, one of 'Lessons from Parents'

87

'Lessons from Parents'

This series is typical of Utamaro's moral lesson prints produced during the Kyôwa Era. Plate 101 shows a woman brushing her teeth in the morning. She is drawn in a diagonal angle across the print and depicted in a considerably realistic way as noted in her expression while holding water in her mouth and in her hair a little dishevelled at the hairline. There is, however, some retrogression in style in this picture when compared with the fullness of those lively beauties created at

Utamaro's peak.

Plate 102 has a long passage of moral teaching which compares a lovely girl with an ugly, old, blind masseur. This composition is typical of Utamaro's later years.

103 —
A Lecher and
a Virgin, one of
'Variegated
Word Blossoms'

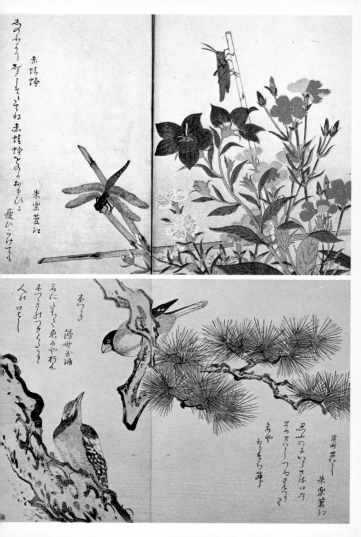

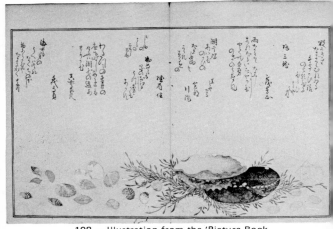

108 — Illustration from the 'Picture Book
of Ebb-Tide Findings'

Book Illustration Prints

When compared with the great volume of single independent pictures, an unexpectedly small number of book illustrations was left by Utamaro. However, in the illustrations of the *Picture Book of Selected Insects, Thousands of Birds,* and the *Picture Book of Ebb-tide Findings* (1788), his keen powers of observation as well as his great sketching talent in realistic painting are fully reflected. The illustrations in the trilogy of comic *tanka* poem books *Crazy Moon Lodge* (1788), *Silver World* (1789), and *Samantabhadra Buddha's Image* (1789) are famous.

The fact that many of Utamaro's illustrations were in books published by Tsutaya Jûzaburô reveals how earnestly this publisher extended his powerful sponsorship to Utamaro even in his earlier days when he had not yet gained fame as an Ukiyoe Beautiful Woman print artist. Another publisher, Kazusaya Chûsuke, printed the picture book *Annual Events in the Yoshiwara Gay Quarters* in 1804, one of Utamaro's last works. This is an illustrated collection of every aspect of Shin-Yoshiwara customs and is regarded as a masterpiece of its kind. Utamaro's illustrations in this book are valuable in studying the general style of his book illustrations.

109 — Illustration from the 'Picture Book of Crazy Moon Lodge'

110 —
Painting titled
'Beauty Changing
Clothes'

94

111 —
Painting
titled
'Standing
Beauty'

112 — Painting titled 'Beauty Cooling Herself'

Paintings

The three pictures introduced in Plates 110-112 are all typical of Utamaro's hand painted works and have been designated Important Art Objects. Plate 110 conveys the feeling of a woman who is relaxing at home with her sash loosened after a summer day's visiting. In Plate 111 delicate lines are drawn to display to advantage the figure of a beautiful woman adjusting her sash on her way to a temple. It is a subtle contrast of the formal and the informal — the formal clothes, the informal posture, the fan in her mouth, the umbrella propped against her legs. The delicately undulating lines give an effect different from that of woodblock prints. Utamaro applies a special technique learned through his experience in woodblock prints to Plate 112 so that the under-garment of the courtesan cooling herself appears through her overgarment of thinner material. This technique was used later by other Japanese painters, such as Uemura Shôen and Itô Shinsui.

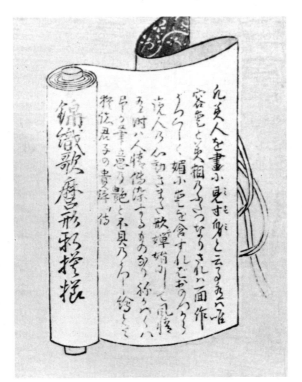

113 — Detail of Title Scroll
from the 'Women in New
Utamaro-Style Costumes' Series

Utamaro's Early Work and His Patron Tsutaya

When one thinks of Ukiyoe portraits, as said earlier, one first thinks of Utamaro. He was extremely popular in his own time and has remained so to this day. A Japanese film titled *Five Women around Utamaro* has been made about his life, and a musical titled *Utamaro* was recently staged in Japan. The name of Utamaro often evokes a somewhat sentimental nostalgia in the Japanese.

Utamaro started his career by doing woodblock prints of actors and book illustrations which were the conventional forms in which Ukiyoe artists of that time published their works. He first used the pen name Utamaro in illustrations for a cheap novel by Shimizu Enjû, who became a good friend. This book was published by Tsutaya Jûzaburô in 1781.

With his pen name Utamaro he began to do prints of beautiful women while continuing the production of actor portraits and book illustrations. Plate 6 is an example of Utamaro's earliest Beautiful Woman prints. The models were low class prostitutes living at the foot of Ueno hill in Yamashita, a gay quarter in the Tokyo of that time. A woman just returned from the bath and another stooping down holding a child on her back and handing him an insect cage are pictured here. These women do not look like ordinary prostitutes and indeed their non-professional appearance was a special characteristic of this pleasure district. They are said to have been menial laborers during the day. Judging from the relation between Utamaro's residence at that time and the location of Yamashita, this work is considered to have been done before 1783, as Utamaro is said to have moved to lodge with the publisher Tsutaya in that year.

Tsutaya Jûzaburô, who Utamaro came in touch with through the introduction of the writer Enjû on the occasion of printing his first work, is regarded as having been a great benefactor to Utamaro. He was born in a brothel in Yoshiwara in 1750 and would have inherited the business, but as he grew up he was not content with being the owner of a whorehouse. In 1772 he opened a bookshop and before long became a publisher by buying the copyright of *A Close-up Look at Yoshiwara.* Succeeding in this publication he bought stock in the business of a local wholesaler on the south side of Tsuyumachi Street and moved there. He gradually became one of Edo's first class publishers. Showing talent both in business and literature and enjoying a wide range of associations, the rising young publisher showed a good understanding of artists as well as a sensitivity to the trends of the time. His eye for genius found Utamaro and Sharaku, and he literally monopolized the works of the writer Santô Kyôden. He showed good judgment as a publisher and encouraged his protégés to do their best work. Santô Kyôden's comic *tanka* poem book *Shikake Bunko* published in 1791 offended the government which had just begun to institute an administrative reform program which included restrictive censorship of artwork. As a result, Santô Kyôden was punished with fifty days in handcuffs and Tsutaya was deprived of half of his household belongings. This unfortunate situation brought Tsutaya to the brink of economic disaster. A plan for publishing a number of very artistic prints by the popular Utamaro and Sharaku was quickly made to recover the sudden loss. Tsutaya died in 1799 at the early age of forty-eight.

Utamaro had by then started producing Beautiful Woman prints. He moved to Yoshiwara and later to Tsuyumachi Street to lodge with Tsutaya. Some say even Utamaro's former residence in Shinobugaoka might have belonged to Tsutaya. With such good support from his patron Utamaro enjoyed the companionship of the many artists and literati who gathered at Tsutaya's house and came to know a life of leisure. Because of his close association with this artistic group it was inevitable that he should come to know many courtesans and prostitutes in that district. It can be said that the taste of pleasure in Yoshiwara later paved the way for Utamaro's success in depicting the people and the way of life of that district. His first-hand experience with life in the gay quarters gave him a deep understanding from which he could draw in portraying the scenes he did. This is why, in spite of the stylization of his work, an intense sense of reality can be felt in his art.

Plate 114 is an example of this period. They were first considered to be part of a series but they are now known to be an independent diptych with the number marked in the

114 — Diptych titled 'Enjoying the
Elegant Fragrance of Flowers'

115 — Diptych titled 'Lovely Prostitues'

corner of each picture. A silvery landscape can be seen through the window. The man at the left, who lingers outside the window, may be Utamaro himself. The standing women passing in the foreground are elegant and graceful but the stooping women in the right-hand print show that Utamaro's technique had not yet been cultivated to a high degree at this time. The distance between the eyes and the facial outlines remind one of the style of Kitao Shigemasa. Thus at this time Utamaro was still greatly influenced by his forerunners. Plate 115 is another example of the influence of Shigemasa. The first part of this diptych is quite well known as a piece in the Matsukata Collection and has been designated an Important Art Object by the Japanese government. Recently the second half of this work was found by chance in Europe. Plate 2 has the same title and may belong to the same series.

Utamaro seems to have drawn his idea for Plate 115 from a group picture by Kiyonaga. Torii Kiyonaga, a contemporary of Utamaro, published during 1783 through 1785, a series which includes a print of a group of men and women enjoying themselves in a bush clover garden. Utamaro drew only women in his bush clover garden but the parallel is striking. In style, however, Utamaro does not take after Kiyonaga but rather Shigemasa who, though not as popular as Kiyonaga at the time, had a mature technique. Utamaro was using detailed drawings of costumes at that time, unlike his later works which have boldly abbreviated designs in the cloth. The use of detailed cloth in his prints may have been a response to the taste of Ukiyoe fans in those days.

Early Beautiful Woman Prints

The famous prints in Plate 116 are owned by the British Museum. When these works are compared with his preceding works, Utamaro's advance in technique becomes obvious, and his image of ideal beauty appears clearly. In these prints he seems to have mastered the characteristics of Ukiyoe wood-block printing and uses a unique technique for the printing of thin cloth as seen in the costumes in the left-hand print and in the image of the woman looking through the man's silk gauze *haori* coat in the right-hand print.

At this time Utamaro treated more general genre subjects than at the time of this brothel series and made use of the

116 — One of 'Four Seasons of Fragrant Flowers in the Gay Quarters'

interest of diptych and triptych works. Utamaro was over thirty when he began to draw women's figures and costumes in his ideal image. While drawing the general customs of the populace, Utamaro made a series called Yoshiwara Niwaka, taking his subjects from an annual festival in the Shin-Yoshiwara pleasure quarter. Plates 8, 9 and 118 show intricate detail in the costumes. Utamaro had gained a great deal of confidence in his work when he did this series. After this series Utamaro began to draw round-faced women according to his image of ideal beauty at that time.

Utamaro became famous for his Beautiful Woman style, but at the same time he did book illustrations like those in the comic *tanka* poem book *Picture Book of Selected Insects*,

117 — Detail from 'Pillow of Poems'

which was published in 1788 and is famous for including a preface referring to Utamaro's relationship with his teacher Toriyama Sekien who was a pioneer in the field of *tanka* poem picture books, which became very popular in the Kansei Era. He was particularly influential in bringing out Utamaro's wonderful talent in the field of realistic sketching. In the same year (1788) the erotic picture book *Pillow of Poems* (see Plate 117) was published. It is considered one of Utamaro's greatest masterpieces. This work consists of twelve large color prints, in which Utamaro's sensual genius is fully demonstrated. This, Utamaro's maiden work of erotic art, was done when he was thirty-five, a little late, one might think, for the first erotic work of an Ukiyoe Beautiful Woman print master, especially when one considers that Kiyonaga drew his first erotic work at twenty and Katsushika Hokusai at twenty-four.

Utamaro then set about producing Beautiful Woman Prints in real earnest, and made diptych and triptych sets of people at leisure like those in Plates 5 and 7. These series were published not only by Tsutaya but also by Tsuruya Kiemon and Fushimiya Zenroku. As a result of Utamaro's vigorous production of Beautiful Woman prints, it is said that Kiyonaga who was the leader of this field in the Tenmei Era was pushed aside by Utamaro and returned to his previous work of painting actor portraits, formerly the main work of Torii school artists.

Utamaro's teacher Sekien died in 1788 and Utamaro soon after that used a seal reading "living independently" on his works in the comic *tanka* poem picture book *Metaphoric Songs* and in *Ebb-tide Findings*. These indicate his confidence as an independent artist. In 1790 when Utamaro was becoming popular, a woman close to him died. Because of the lack of biographical data on Utamaro's life we do not know his exact relationship to this woman, but we know that he was deeply

獅子

さ川屋
あいと

哥麿

118 — Lion Dancers, one of 'Entertainers at the
Niwaka Festival in the Gay Quarters'

affected by her death. Also it was at this time that Matsudaira Sadanobu began a program of purges intended to reconstruct the government regime and reform Japanese society.

Origin of Beautiful Woman Close-up Portraits

Thus Utamaro had to deal with both political opression and private grief in a short span of time. Nevertheless it was at this time that he originated a new style of Beautiful Woman portrait -- the close-up. He is thought to have taken the idea from the style of actor portraits done by the Katsukawa school. In the Beautiful Woman close-ups Utamaro uses the technique of a crushed mica background to further enhance the beauty of the model and he reduced the number of lines to the minimum, using the juxtaposition of different colors without outlines. He actually used only a small variety of colors in subtle shades and created a new, very delicate and muted type of woodblock print.

He wrote his signature in Plates 17-20 and 22-25 somewhat whimsically as "painted by physiognomy reader Utamaro." He also tried to convey expressions of thought or emotion as seen in Plates 22 and 24 in these series often using humorous titles. He made single figure prints of renowned beauties of Edo at that time like Ochie of Koise-ya Teahouse, Okita of Naniwa-ya Teahouse, Oseyo of Hirano-ya Teahouse, Ohisa of Takashima-ya Teahouse, and Toyohina of Tomimoto-ya Teahouse. The former three were famous tea shop hostesses, Ohisa worked in a famous shop to attract customers with her beauty, and Toyohina was a famous singer. These are not real portraits of the individual women, but are drawn rather uniformly according to Utamaro's ideal image. Therefore, they all seem to look alike

119 — Deeply Pining for Love,
one of 'Poems of Love'

but if you examine the faces carefully you can distinguish differences in their features with slight changes in the lines of eyes, noses and eyebrows. In order to emphasize the facial structure of women of beauty, Utamaro used a new style of close-up print that shows only the head, as seen in *Collection of Dancers* and *Poems of Love* series.

In Plate 119, the engraver's high craftsmanship in the handling of the hair must be applauded along with Utamaro's sketching talent in its contribution to the total effect of this print. Utamaro often used crimson mica for the background instead of white or black mica to produce a total coloring effect which makes the model's face more striking. He also used backgrounds of bright, warm yellow or gray spots. Probably because of the great success of these close-ups he did not do any book illustrations during 1791 and 1792.

The feature Utamaro tried to stress in his Beautiful Woman close-ups changed from ideal beauty to beauty of expression. This tendency seems to be a response to the mood of the general populace who, after the retirement of Matsudaira Sadanobu and his oppressive policies, reacted with a freedom from inhibitions in their expression of feelings and emotions. Utamaro sketched women's beauty from many aspects in his *Maidens of the Hours* and *Six Tama Rivers* series. By not using outlines for the face, Utamaro succeeded in presenting a sense of soft and fair skin in addition to presenting his ideal of the beauty of expression. This technique shows to advantage the juxtaposition of the crushed yellow background and the white of the paper, a special paper used particularly for Ukiyoe woodblock prints. Utamaro also began to use darker color for costumes than in his previous works. In this series Utamaro's intention to present women's beauty more by the juxtaposition of color planes than by drawing outlines is very successful.

Utamaro endeavored to use colors to invoke a sense of solidity and weight. This led, however, to a certain finickiness in the use of color and his figures became a little stereotyped compared to his former work. This might be a consequence of the hasty mass production of these Beautiful Woman close-ups to answer the demand for them which amounted to a boom in the field of art.

Resumption of Full Length Works/Chôbunsai Eishi

Utamaro returned to the production of full length prints and group prints in the middle of the Kansei Era. Unlike his close-ups the prominent feature of these figure prints is the beauty of posture and costume. In the group print, composition becomes the important element. The number of prints of beautifully, brightly dressed courtesans of the Shin-Yoshiwara quarter began to increase in Utamaro's works during this time.

In the series, which displays full length figures of beautiful courtesans who contended for status, Utamaro uses a characteristic composition technique which is often used in Oriental art in which blank space is utilized. One of Utamaro's characteristic stylizations can be seen in the idealistic delineation of the drawn-up knees. Such a stylization becomes more obvious in his triptych prints. Plate 120 is an unusual double triptych set joining three pieces on a bridge to another three portraying the scene under the same bridge forming quite a large overall scene. It is a novel idea but the delineation of the under-the-bridge pieces is a little too fussy and the merits of his best sets are not fully demonstrated here. It is noted in this example that full length figures have been lengthened to become tall, slender, small-headed people. Such slender figures are not the

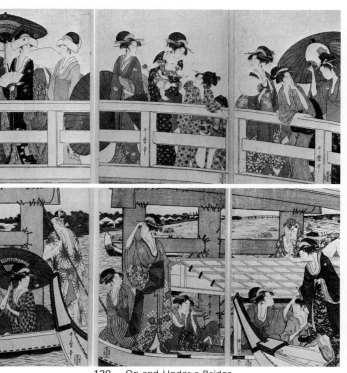

120 — On and Under a Bridge

result of a direct development of Utamaro's style but rather remind us of the style of Beautiful Woman prints by Chôbunsai Eishi, who was one of the most competitive of Utamaro's contemporaries. Plate 121 is a typical work by Eishi from his *Beauties in the Gay Quarters* series. It shows Takigawa of Ôgiya Teahouse dressed in a gorgeous overcloak. Her tall, slender figure with a very small head (only a twelfth of the total body length) is typical of Eishi.

It is not known for what reasons Eishi gave up his position as a direct vassal of the Shogun, for which he received an annual stipend, to become an Ukiyoe artist. Eishi had studied the painting of the Kanô school which was regarded as the orthodox drawing school throughout the Edo Period. He titled his works *Eishi's Cartoons*. With his Kanô school training background Eishi followed Kiyonaga's style of Ukiyoe Beautiful Woman art and developed his tall, slender, small-headed women and their elaborate costumes to an exaggerated form. Perhaps partly due to his early career in orthodox art forms, he was well supported by a class of fans different from those who supported Utamaro. Thus Utamaro and Eishi shared the popularity of the Kansei Era as the two leaders of the Ukiyoe art world.

It is rather surprising that Utamaro seems to have been influenced by Eishi's style when he made the very tall, thin beauties in *Twelve Hours in the Gay Quarters* (Plates 66-77 and Plate 120).

Twelve Hours in the Gay Quarters displays the daily lives of Shin-Yoshiwara prostitutes in twelve pieces, one for every two hours. Both *The Hour of the Rat* and *The Hour of the Ox* seen in plates 66 and 67 have such exaggeratedly tall models. The composition of *The Hour of the Rat* is well-balanced by the girl folding a kimono, which helps making the standing woman more impressive. *The Hour of the Ox* is especially notable for

121 — CHÔBUNSAI EISHI Woman in a Teahouse,
one of 'Beauties in the Gay Quarters'

the fine composition of the dishevelled figure of a woman just getting up to go to the toilet and for the idea of an upside-down sandal, which subtly conveys the haste and lack of order in the lives of the women living in pleasure districts. Utamaro shows his keen powers of observation and excellent talent in composition especially in this series. He places a woman just out of the bath and a girl serving tea both leaning backward together giving them a slightly bowlike posture in *The Hour of the Serpent* (Plate 69).

The lines of composition in *The Hour of the Horse* (Plate 73) also follow body postures as a woman bends forward to show a letter to a courtesan who leans backward a little. A servant was placed behind them to give a sense of solidity and balance to the print. Utamaro has also succeeded in giving a sense of solidity to the picture as a whole in *The Hour of the Ram* (Plates 70 and 122) by arranging the three women in a diagonal line from upper left to lower right. The darker colors of the costumes of the women on either side of the middle make a contrast with the pink of the middle woman's costumes to heighten the effect of depth. The prints from *The Hour of the Ram* through *The Hour of the Boar* (Plates 70-75) present the business activities of the life of the prostitutes. The young servant girl in *The Hour of the Dog* (Plate 77) who is facing the front and is being whispered to by the courtesan has a precocious look, a common characteristic of girls living in the pleasure world. In *The Hour of the Boar* in contrast to the innocent look of the servant who has begun to doze during a drinking party, the dauntless manner of the courtesan offering a drink demonstrates her consciousness of herself as a professional entertainer. This series presents various aspects of Utamaro's artistic talent and technique.

122 — Hour of the Ram (2 p.m.), one of
'Twelve Hours in the Gay Quarters'

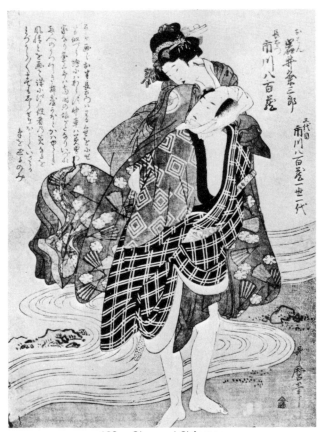

123 — Ohan and Chôemon

A very popular artist, Utamaro in those days had a great volume of orders from more than forty first-class publishers. There was so much demand for his work that he was obliged to produce a great quantity of work in a short time resulting in some rather shoddy pieces and "formula" scenes.

He was then equal in popularity with his powerful rival Eishi, the young Utagawa Toyokuni I (1769-1825), and his colleague Utagawa Toyohiro (1773-1828), and that singular genius Katsushika Hokusai (famous for landscape prints), all of whom were just beginning to enter the art world. A contemporary of Utamaro, Tôshûsai Sharaku, who drew very impressive actor portraits suddenly disappeared from the public eye without his art having been appreciated by the world. Seeing how Sharaku had been shunted aside by all the new and great talent appearing, Utamaro must have become a little uneasy wondering what might happen if people were to get tired of his prints. His powerful patron Tsutaya, of course, would still have supported him. Perhaps this is why Utamaro writes praise of himself as an artist in the letter which the woman is reading in Plate 93 and many other prints. Perhaps these declarations of confidence really concealed his sense of uneasiness in allowing himself to mass produce so many pieces. Plate 123 is an Utamaro work illustrating a scene from the Kabuki play *Ohan and Chôemon* which was staged in 1803. Utamaro adds his personal words in the blank space of the picture: "My 'Ohan and Chôemon' is not the kind of portrait which tries only to emphasize bad features. Chûsha, the actor doing Chôemon, is from a family of handsome men and Kumesaburô, the actor portraying the courtesan Ohan, is a wonderful female impersonator. How beautifully they both act. I wished to draw their lovely faces so that the beauty of Edo actors becomes known throughout the country. For this reason have I taken up my pen." The first sentence of this statement could be regarded as an allusion to Toyokuni I who had discouraged Sharaku from drawing actors and was planning to monopolize the popularity of this genre. It can also be interpreted as a demonstration of the superiority of Utamaro's idealism over those realistic sketches usually seen in actor portraits.

From the middle of the Kansei Era he made pictures of drama scenes taking themes mainly from double suicide stories in the Bunraku Puppet *Jôruri* drama. *Dramas of Loving Couples* and *Types of Love and Devotion* are series of this type.

Besides taking material from dramas Utamaro also published works treating women's work in the series *Women's Skills* and *Twelve Skills of Women*. Another is *Twelve Customs of Beautiful Woman.* These show women at various tasks at different times of the day using the same time counting style as in *Twelve Hours in the Gay Quarters,* for example, *A Mistress at The Hour of the Rat, Shrine Maiden at The Hour of the Horse. Maidservants at the Hour of the Hare* (Plate 124) shows the social position of the women. As these women are drawn according to Utamaro's ideal type of beauty, they all appear as fresh and lovely as tradesmen's wives. Utamaro deliberately portrayed them so because of the government's strict censorship of Ukiyoe print publication.

In the series titled *Woman of the Mountain and Kintarô,* Utamaro treats the subject of motherly love. This woman (*Yamanba*), in Japanese legend, is a mountain prostitute who found baby Kintarô and reared him. Kintarô is a super-strong hero in Japanese legend. Production of this series is considered to have been started about the middle of the Kansei Era. Utamaro drew pictures with this theme increasingly during the Kyôwa Era (1801-1804) and also did other similar works treating the daily lives of mothers and small children.

124 — Maidservants at the Hour of the Hare (6 a.m.),
one of 'Twelve Customs of Beautiful Women'

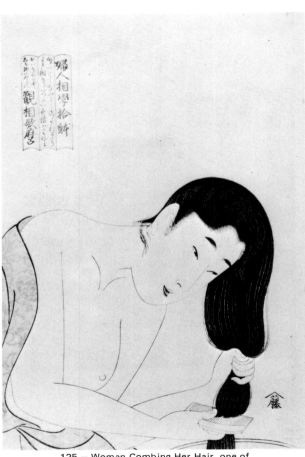

婦人相學拾躰

觀相教學

**125 — Woman Combing Her Hair, one of
'Ten Types of Women'**

Along with depicting parental love Utamaro wrote tedious pedantic passages in the blank spaces of some prints as seen in Plates 100-103. In the meantime with a view to propping up his popularity he reused the name of his once hit series *Ten Types of Women*, which had so heightened his fame. Plate 125 is an example of this series. In this print Utamaro delineated the model's voluptuous physical beauty by a minimum of fine lines outlining her body. This indicates that Utamaro's skill had not declined and also that good cooperation between painter and engraver was very important in producing such master works.

Utamaro, conscious of his somewhat declining popularity due to the poor quality of his hastily produced works, was struggling to regain his past fame when in 1804 an event almost fatal to his artistic life occurred. Plate 126 incurred the government's wrath and Utamaro was condemned to three days in jail plus fifty days in handcuffs. The subject was drawn from Okada Gyokuzan's *Picture Book of the Life of Hideyoshi* which had gained fame in Osaka and was construed by the authorities as critical of Hideyoshi's character and thereby also a reflection on the present government. At the inquiry Utamaro revealed that he had taken his subject from Gyokuzan's book. As a result the sale of that book was prohibited in Osaka. Utamaro reportedly related that he deeply regretted printing such a print and apologized for having caused his publishers such serious trouble.

It seems that Utamaro was very deeply affected by this incident. Publishers, noticing his decline, quickly placed orders for his prints for fear that he would soon go into a more serious decline. He worked industriously at his drawing and made a great effort to answer requests for his works. However, his Beautiful Woman prints after this shock changed so greatly that

seeing a variety of his post-arrest prints one may well feel they were not really Utamaro's work.

His later works are difficult to distinguish from those done by Utamaro II. Another opinion is that the works of Utamaro II are distinguishable by a slight difference in the signature. However, there is no certain and established way to distinguish the latter works of Utamaro and those of Utamaro II.

126 — Toyotomi Hideyoshi and His Five Wives
at a Cherry Blossom Viewing Party

In spite of this final decline of the quality of his works, Utamaro remains one of the major artists of the world. His skill in composition, his technical superiority in expression, and his creative talent in introducing novel ideas and superior print techniques certainly have not been surpassed by any other artist in this medium — even today.

127 — Hairdressing, one of 'Black Moon-Shaped
Eyebrows on the Six Tama Rivers'

HOIKUSHA COLOR BOOKS
ENGLISH EDITIONS

Book Size 4″×6″

COLORED ILLUSTRATIONS FOR NATURALISTS

Text in Japanese, with index in Latin or English.

First Issues (Book Size 6″ × 8″)

1. BUTTERFLIES of JAPAN
2. INSECTS of JAPAN vol.1
3. INSECTS of JAPAN vol.2
4. SHELLS of JAPAN vol.1
5. FISHES of JAPAN vol.1
6. BIRDS of JAPAN
7. MAMMALS of JAPAN
8. SEA SHORE ANIMALS of JAPAN
9. GARDEN FLOWERS vol.1
10. GARDEN FLOWERS vol.2
11. ROSES and ORCHIDS
12. ALPINE FLORA of JAPAN vol.1
13. ROCKS
14. ECONOMIC MINERALS
15. HERBACEOUS PLANTS of JAPAN vol.1
16. HERBACEOUS PLANTS of JAPAN vol.2
17. HERBACEOUS PLANTS of JAPAN vol.3
18. SEAWEEDS of JAPAN
19. TREES and SHRUBS of JAPAN
20. EXOTIC AQUARIUM FISHES vol.1
21. MOTHS of JAPAN vol.1
22. MOTHS of JAPAN vol.2
23. FUNGI of JAPAN vol.1
24. PTERIDOPHYTA of JAPAN
25. SHELLS of JAPAN vol.2
26. FISHES of JAPAN vol.2
27. EXOTIC AQUARIUM FISHES vol.2
28. ALPINE FLORA of JAPAN vol.2
29. FRUITS
30. REPTILES and AMPHIBIANS of JAPAN
31. ECONOMIC MINERALS vol.2
32. FRESHWATER FISHES of JAPAN
33. GARDEN PLANTS of the WORLD vol.1
34. GARDEN PLANTS of the WORLD vol.2
35. GARDEN PLANTS of the WORLD vol.3
36. GARDEN PLANTS of the WORLD vol.4
37. GARDEN PLANTS of the WORLD vol.5
38. THE FRESHWATER PLANKTON of JAPAN
39. MEDICINAL PLANTS of JAPAN

40. VEGETABLE CROPS of JAPAN

41. FARM ANIMALS of JAPAN

42. FUNGI of JAPAN vol.2

43. SHELLS of the WORLD vol.1

44. SHELLS of the WORLD vol.2

45. THE MARINE PLANKTON of JAPAN

46. EARLY STAGES of JAPANESE MOTHS vol.1

47. EARLY STAGES of JAPANESE MOTHS vol.2

48. FOSSILS

49. WOODY PLANTS of JAPAN vol.1

50. WOODY PLANTS of JAPAN vol.2

51. BRYOPHYTES of JAPAN

52. LICHEN FLORA of JAPAN

53. NATURALIZED PLANTS of JAPAN

54. DISEASES and PESTS of CULTIVATED TREES and SHRUBS

55. DISEASES and PESTS of FLOWERS and VEGETABLES

Second Issues (Book Size 7″ × 10″)

1. BUTTERFLIES of FORMOSA

2. EARLY STAGES of JAPANESE BUTTERFLIES vol.1

3. EARLY STAGES of JAPANESE BUTTERFLIES vol.2

4. SPIDERS of JAPAN

5. THE PLANKTON of JAPANESE COASTAL WATERS

6. BIRDS′ LIFE in JAPAN vol.1

7. BIRDS′ LIFE in JAPAN vol.2

8. CAGE BIRDS

9. WORLD FOLK COSTUMES

10. ATLAS of WOOD

11. PLANTS of JAPAN in their Environment

12. SPRING FLORA of SIKKIM HIMALAYA

Third Issues (Book Size 6″ × 8″)

1. INSECTS′ LIFE in JAPAN vol.1 Longicorn Beetles

2. INSECTS′ LIFE in JAPAN vol.2 Dragonflies

3. INSECTS′ LIFE in JAPAN vol.3 Butterflies

SHELLS
OF
THE
WESTERN
PACIFIC
IN
COLOR

Book Size 7″×10″

⟨vol. I⟩ by Tetsuaki Kira
(304 pages, 72 in color)
⟨vol. II⟩ by Tadashige Habe
(304 pages, 66 in color)

FISHES
OF
JAPAN
IN
COLOR

Book Size 7″×10″

by Toshiji Kamohara
(210 pages, 64 in color)